Landscape
with
Female
Figure

Landscape
with
Female
Figure

new and selected poems, 1982–2012

Andrea Hollander

pittsburgh

Autumn House Press Staff

Editor-in-Chief and Founder: Michael Simms
Managing Editor: Caroline Tanski
Production Editor: Adrienne Block
Co-Founder: Eva-Maria Simms
Community Outreach Director: Michael Wurster
Fiction Editors: Sharon Dilworth, John Fried
Assistant Editors: Giuliana Certo, Christine Stroud
Media Consultant: Jan Beatty
Publishing Consultant: Peter Oresick
Tech Crew Chief: Michael Milberger

PENNSYLVANIA
COUNCIL
ON THE

ARTS

Autumn House Press receives state arts funding support through a grant from the Pennsylvania Council on the Arts, a state agency funded by the Commonwealth of Pennsylvania, and the National Endowment for the Arts, a federal agency.

ISBN: 978-1-932870-85-5
Library of Congress Control Number: 2013932273

For

Susan Elizabeth Fiser Barham

1947–2013

I have opened my windows.
I have swung the door
way back on its hinges.
And I am no longer careful.
Once I leave the house
I might be someone else
returning.

Contents

Landscape with Female Figure: New Poems (2006–2012)

From *Woman in the Painting* (2006)

From *The Other Life* (2001)

From *House Without a Dreamer* (1993)

✳

Landscape
with
Female
Figure

new poems, 2006–2012

Finches or Sparrows

First the wheezing wind, and then I saw them,
hundreds it seemed, yellow and brown
and yellow-brown. I wondered how they knew
to fly in such parallel lines and so fast and
together simultaneously from the shaking hickory
the wind had disturbed, straight out from the tree
so fast I couldn't tell which they were, finches
or sparrows. Then the wind hesitated
for a moment the way in that final bed
my mother seemed to, her chest still, breath
suddenly gone for a moment, but actually
held in—savored, I thought later—
the way her body had tried to hold me
a little longer, the cord that had kept me
alive now wrapped around my throat,
pulling me back the way all those years later
I wanted to pull her back. And now, outside,
the wind wheezing again like her breath
escaping from her chest. There was nothing
I could do to make her keep it, those birds—
finches, sparrows—moving so fast
I could not tell which. Then the wheezing
stopped, the wild, invisible gods released them,
and I saw I had been mistaken: All at once
they dropped, fluttering to the ground,
nothing but leaves, yellow and brown.

New Year's Day

I rise early and remember
what my long-dead grandmother said

when my long-dead grandfather
disappointed her: *You reap what you sow.*

When I was too young to understand
that words could be sod laid over

something dark and unuttered
I understood only that she believed

he had caused his own failures
and she blamed him.

As the years passed I too
failed, disappointed myself and others,

and each time could hear her voice—
reap, sow, reap, sow.

And so this first morning of the new year
I raise a nearly empty glass left

from last night's merriment and make a wish
for all good things to be sown,

while the promised snow
scatters its solemn white flakes

and I picture my grandfather again,
his stained ties, his black scuffed shoes

I polished whenever I stayed with them,
his lost jobs, his apologies,

the apron he wore after she died,
my grandfather poised at the sink

—I'd never seen him there before—
a man in a woman's apron

with no one to apologize to,
nothing to apologize for.

Photograph of Her Grandmother as a Young Woman

for Miriam Mörsel Nathan

If only it had been passed down
the way it should have been passed down
grandmother to mother to daughter

If she could have known the color of the dress
she guessed might have been yellow
but pale like the tulips in her garden
and not the sewn-on stars

If it had been passed down
in its frame where it must have stood with a family
of photographs on a credenza
in the house they left
when they were told to leave
to leave everything as it was
and go

If only
they had not been told to go

and it was only
a story passed down
grandmother to mother to daughter
hand to hand and not by a stranger
who had searched
to find her

a story passed down
a typical boring story like anyone's

blameless and sweet

Milkweed

In those days I walked to school. And afterwards,
sauntering because I could, no rush to reach
home, no one worried if the door opened
and closed behind me ten, twenty minutes late,
sometimes I took the path
through the little parcel of woods,
down the hill, across the narrow stream,
wild patches of milkweed along it, then out
to a green expanse that belonged to no one.

Often I would loiter, brushing the weeds
with my fingertips, my mind
drifting among the spent ones, loving
the way they appeared so lifeless at first,
their dry, slender stalks motionless,
loving the way they kept so still
until I touched them, and the way then
with such ease they would open, let go
their silky, milk-white secrets.

I wondered how long they had waited like that,
wanting but not revealing their desire—
as years later I would do, as maybe you too
have done, not understanding you *could* want,
not knowing you could be more
than a stalk by a stream at the edge
of anything.

Kenmore Hotel, 1965

And when she realizes he expects her
to undress, to lie down on the hotel bed
next to him, or under, "God forgive me,"
she whispers to herself under her breath,
for agreeing to meet him here the night before
the dorms reopen. She told her parents
she had to take the only train that got her
back on time. Now she stands at the window,
her new wool coat folded over the back
of the only chair in the room, the pearls
he gave her newly circling her neck.
A brittle January snow has taken hold.
Through the window she hears the wind
whisper its bitter *no*, its bitter *yes*. Traffic
on the street below barely moves at all.
The glow from the neon Citgo sign
tints the room blue, then red, then blue again.
All night she lies beside him in her clothes,
neither sleeping nor speaking.

Desire

She was looking for a way in.
He was the one. Doubt

surfaced, as it always did.
She pushed it down, stood on it,

a rock
that made her taller.

*

The way the trees stood
in the all-day rain, the gray

light around them, the way
she peered through

as if through windows,
as if a forest were a house

and all you had to do was enter.

*

Inside, a low moan—
cello maybe, or oboe.

*

What does it take to ignore the end
of the story that pulls you to it like a magnet

against your desire? To finish instead
at the penultimate page,

the wanting and wanting and wanting.

Other

As in *odd, out of context, unexpected*
(meaning the woman you only glimpsed
  when you thought you glimpsed him with an *other*)

As in *hand*, if not on one, then on the other
  meaning nothing one could hold
  but only a thing we weigh
  that has no volume and cannot be placed
  in any hand
  but nevertheless
  weighs you down

As in *additional* or *further*, meaning him and one other person
  meaning the person you glimpsed
  when you thought you glimpsed him

As in *different* or *distinct*—
  "Did you expect him any other way?"

Or something vague, something you cannot distinguish
  from something else, as in *something or other*

As in *the others*—the ones who no longer matter
  or the ones who do

Or singular, as in "You are my other, my only"
  meaning the one who couldn't be the one
  you glimpsed with another

As in *otherwise*, meaning
    "I can't go on, other than with you."

Or you might be wise to reconsider
and simply ask, "Was that you I glimpsed the other day?"
    (You needn't add "with another woman.")
    But then he'll ask and you'll be at each other's throats

Unless they were made for each other
    (the way it looked)

You could just turn the other cheek
and wait for the other shoe to drop

On the other hand, on another day
the shoe could be on the other foot.

Every Time Her Husband Climbs a Ladder—

first the framing, then the roof beams,
then the plywood, shingles, edging,
roof vent, and now the gutters—
she wants to pray him down. Not
so he hears her and complains
that builders cost money
they don't have—they agreed
he'd do it all himself.

But sometimes she slips and says out loud,
"Be careful," and he gives her
the look of his that says
I love you but please don't tell me
the obvious (not that she hasn't
saved them a few times on highways)—
as if it were nothing much
to haul a 4 x 8 sheet of plywood
up a sixteen-foot ladder and lift it
over his head and slam it onto rafters,
nail it in place as he squats on the roof,
then goes down again for another.

"We take care with big things, but take
small ones for granted," her father always
warned. "That's when accidents happen."
Perhaps it's her father's voice she raises
when her mouth opens against
her better self. It's like that game
she played as a kid, not stepping

on cracks, believing a child
would make a difference in a world
where her mother could die of cancer
even though her father's a doctor.
As if saying something now
would force the gods
this time to listen.

Retrospective

I'm not the only one to feel the loneliness
of the stark white house with the mansard roof
in one of Hopper's paintings, the house
facing railway tracks that span the canvas,
a bland, treeless landscape covering the rest.
And so the eye regards the framed space, scouting
for evidence—perhaps a smear of paint to suggest
the shadow of some bird (even a vulture would mean
something small and alive had escaped us).
We do not doubt the season: summer. Time of day:
high noon, point of sharpest light—
which should make the scene seem
important, vibrant, but it doesn't.

If the body is indeed a temple, the hand
of a painter signifies the spirit
speaking out, Hopper saying, You
have forsaken me, meaning perhaps God.
But we who stop before it, enter
its landscape. In its harsh light
we imagine only freight trains clatter by
releasing steam and soot. We step
as close as the guard will allow
to see if there isn't someone
standing in the shadow of an upstairs window
peering down at the man who day after day
stood before an easel in the unrelenting
glare and heat, as we stand before it now,
its terrible blankness drawing us in.

American Gothic

Called in from the field to pose
in farm clothes instead of dressing up
as they would have for a portrait
if they had known how long
a woman like me
would stand at this frame and study
their faces, the lines around their eyes,
trying to decipher any messages
hidden there.

Oh, I know they're not really
who they're meant to seem,
that Wood persuaded his dentist
and sweet-talked his own sister,
now forever famous as people
they're not.

Perhaps we're never who we seem to be,
pitchfork in hand or dentist's tool,
dressed in overalls or painter's smock,
or, as my husband was,
in the cashmere sweater I'd bought him,
smiling and wide-eyed for the picture I took
the day before I caught him.

Portrait with Purple Shroud

Portrait because a woman over sixty
should be mysterious
not hidden—

Purple because the myth of color
says magenta, periwinkle,
the bruise I kept hidden

yellowing now, not yelling
the way I couldn't
until I could.

Whom will he bed
while I'm away?

Shroud although nothing
can be hidden
even when draped, wrapped.

When I go back
I'll sleep on the sun porch.

I was afraid
until I understood I was afraid.

Blue

I take the laundry down from the line
and the line speaks to me, gray line
breaking the sky in two, each half blue
but one pale, the other darker
than the ceramic bowl that broke
this morning as I lifted it from the table
after my cereal, without a hint
of what would happen next. I lifted it
and it just split, the dribble of milk
suddenly puddling on the Formica
like evidence, like white blood.

I stood holding two useless half-
truths in my hands, two blue
half-truths bluer than your blue eyes
I grew so used to looking into.
The break was clean, inevitable—
hidden beneath the glaze
a fissure that would someday
crack the bowl apart. If you
were reading this now you'd say,
She's talking about us again in her usual
talk-about-something-else way.

Taffeta

In her hospital bed, my mother talks
about next month's holiday, her favorite, she says,

ringing in the season. She wants taffeta,
red taffeta—she loves the feel of it. She loves

whirring it through her Singer. And as she speaks
I can picture her at the sewing table

or on the couch hemming
while Lawrence Welk introduces another polka.

A gown, she says, with ruffles.
And I promise to shop for patterns, bring back

samples of all the possibilities. As I say this
I wonder if she knows

she'll never leave this bed. She's only
fifty-one. She loves figs in summer,

and at this time of year pomegranates.
She taught us how to eat them:

hidden in each white pocket a throng of crimson seeds
pungent on the tongue. Now

her eyes droop a little, and she asks
for water. I start to hand her the plastic cup

but have to hold it while she sips.
My father clears his throat. He's been rubbing her feet

since we got here. This will be her last day
but we don't know it. I'm thinking of the sheen

of taffeta, the way the bolt will roll out
onto the cutting table.

Afterwards

He moved as if through water.
As if odors were so distant
they might not exist.

On his plate the bones
of a trout lifted too easily
from its flesh. On the street,

red light or green, even amber,
always about to change and never
enough time.

And what was he to do
about the girl at the crosswalk
jabbering at her dog,

or on the ball field
near the cemetery
that boy's face turned

at the wrong moment
the wrong direction?
Nothing could be stopped.

All of it too quick.
Even the sun like an old dog
chained to the gate post

pulling him against his will
through every day—
and every night the moon.

On My Father's 87th Birthday

My stepmother cradles the receiver
to his ear and tells him I've called
to wish him a happy birthday.
"Happy birthday," he says,
"happy birthday," a child imitating
his parents' noises, wanting to cause
more of the pleasure he sees
on their grownup faces.
"No, Dad, it's *your* birthday," I say.
"Happy birthday to *you!*" Then silence.
Then my stepmother's worn voice,
her apology, as if his disease
were *her* doing, something *she'd*
brought into the family, the way
children convince their parents
to take in some sorrowful mongrel,
its mange never quite healing, its hearing
so damaged after its previous owner
kicked its head that when you call,
it turns in confusion one
wrong direction after another,
the poor thing forever drooling,
begging to be let out, let in,
sometimes peeing at the door,
my father grumbling,
"What a mistake—
somebody should have
put it down years ago."

The Inconsolable

after William Meredith

Touching his forehead, she was like the beam
of moonlight that found its way through the lace
curtains, brightening his finally calm face
that night, making of it something that seemed
holy, or would have if she were someone
who believed. And for that moment she did
believe that the streak of moonlight had come
as if to anoint him just as he died
in what had been their room and now a place
where in daylight hours she had come to him,
taken over for the nurse, fed him,
changed his soiled clothes. In this place
now, her hand smooth upon his still warm skin,
what would you call how she feels touching him?

Natural Causes

The track was hidden by a line
of junipers. All afternoon
children played in the gazebo.
The sound of a train surprised me.
I sorted, packed, labeled cartons.
Children played. Now and then a train
muffled their laughter. I packed, swept.
Sunlight shifted across floorboards,
climbed stacks of cartons, entered
my father's bed with its folded clothes,
piles of books. Trains shuttled by,
light squinted through trees,
voices diminished, left.
Night arrived. I tried to sleep.
Thanked the trains for their thunder,
the children, in their own beds,
for their concentrated play. Trees
for trying to hide the track,
the track for leading away.

Quickly

After she read one of my poems about my father's death,
my goddaughter said she was glad my life was marked
only by the "more or less natural losses" of my parents.
"And let it stay that way," I said. Quickly. Almost before
she'd gotten her last word out. As if saying so this fast
could prevent another death. Like those experiments
in high school science class: You would fill the vial
with one invisible element and all the air would leave.
Nothing else could enter, and nothing could displace it.

Large Boulder Above Honey River

If you look closely: a tiny crack
in the stone that to an ant must seem
a chasm. Closer, you see a procession
of scurrying insects smaller than ants.

Think of winters there. Think
of their intricate dwellings,
their roads impossible to detect,
tunnels thin as hairs

weaving into their deep cities
of blackness where the roots
of this old sycamore help
to open the earth. The river

isn't really a river but a creek
my grown son named as a boy.
The name stuck. Ever since the ice storm,
I don't come much. Too many

toppled trees, the difficult climb
down from the cliff. Thick
tangles of briar. Snakes.
But today I've come anyway.

In part for memory, in part
to listen again,
to experience something
humans didn't make or say.

A hawk hovers for a moment
on the other side, then rises
and circles away. A single branch
of the sycamore shivers above me,

likely a squirrel I cannot see.
Then for a moment, nothing—
no movement, no sound. This far
from the house, no news to read about,

no radio to turn off. No terrorists. No wars.

Wood Thrush

I'm walking the same dirt road to the mailbox,
a half-mile uphill and not a single house

unless you count the one a wood thrush is building
in some tree I can't spot in these overgrown woods.

I've read such birds are monogamous
and it's the female that builds the nest.

This one keeps flitting in and out of the tree-line,
debris of one kind or another stringing from her beak.

Females don't sing. It's males whose songs are so beautiful
one species is called the nightingale thrush.

I keep trudging up this hill every afternoon
hoping the mail lady has come in her blue jeep.

One day last week I waited for an hour. She took my letter
but gave back only an ad for a washing machine.

It doesn't surprise me that the male can sing
two notes at once.

At the top of the hill I see she's late again:
the little red flag I raised this morning is still up.

I wait in the shade of a nearby sycamore.
Behind me a pair of birds argues

the way we used to: trying reason first, then
pleading, screeching, until one of them thrashes away.

Europeans consider the wood thrush a vagrant.
It's been weeks this time and still you're not back.

Wander

What we don't know we don't know,
so accept it. If your mother wandered

when your father was stationed in France
during the war before you were born,

before you were even conceived, so be it.
No matter what her sister told you

years later, after your mother died,
what does this matter now?

Your job anyway is to be the daughter,
to stay open to where you are,

your ear toward the glistening insects
that draw your eye to the wild azaleas

pushing their pale pink selves out of
the limestone ledge just over the edge

of the bluff where your house sits.
What you don't know

you will never know. Look instead
at the fluttering pink blossoms, at the lichen

stuck to the limestone ledge beneath them.
Look at the pale thumbprint of the moon

in the pale afternoon sky. The house is nearly
empty now, nearly no longer yours—

tables and chairs sold, couches and beds
given away, trash dumped, books and dishes

boxed and stacked for the truck
that's on its way. Everything is somewhere

else now, intact or scattered. It doesn't matter.
More than once your father wrote

from the field hospital about the nurses.
What was it like to read those letters?

These insects must be honeybees heavying
with nectar—so many lifting in and out

of the wild azaleas you can almost smell their
desire. Wild like your mother's may have been.

Like your husband's was. But you don't know
anything. You can sit on the porch

of this emptying house and think
whatever you think. You never apologized

for your own lies. Your husband apologized
too much. Even then the moon slept on its side,

its good ear deep in its pillow.
Your job was to be the wife and mother,

the daughter. To be whatever you are now.
The moon has its own job. The house

will fill again. Perhaps you are tired
of watching the bees. Of noticing how

the petals of the azaleas strain upward
to right themselves after the bees

have finished with them. Tired
of the questions that repeat themselves

like the fat predictable moon, and the doubt
that manages, no matter what the truth is,

to never run out.

Flight

Six miles up these clouds hide everything.
Not even a glimpse of green lawns or trees,
strings of rooftops bent toward skinny little roads.

In the poem I just read, a woman has been found out,
though she doesn't yet know it. I want to save
the man in the poem from what happens next.

He's right, of course, about what she's done.
Did you ever do a thing like that?
And have a lot to lose, a lot to explain?

For months the man didn't suspect.
Now he cannot forget. He imagines his wife
in another man's car, another man's bed.

He imagines the painting above it, clouds
billowing over cornflowers. He tries not to think
about the other man's hands, or his wife's hands,

her late key in the lock, her gray eyes
that will not look at him. He curses
the moon. I close the book,

raise my seat-back,
secure the tray table to its upright
and locked position.

My plane lowers into clouds, gray
as the woman's eyes. Into rain.
It's the man whose pain I feel.

Into more rain. Onto the wet tarmac.

In Their Bed

Her mistake was believing

when he said it was the only time
when he said never again

the way his face was solemn when he said it
earnest when he said it the second time

when he faced her in bed
the way the next day the bed

the way the next day the bed looked
made the way she'd left it

Her mistake was believing

the way she left it
the way she lifted the pillow to her face
the way she scrutinized the sheets
the way his face in bed
the way he said again never again
the way she wanted to check again
the way she again and again
the way again and again she

whatever he said
the made bed
the solemn face
earnest again

the second again
the only time
pillow and sheets
face in bed
check again
the way she left
whatever he said
he said
believing

Question

for (and after) John Brehm

I've been reading the poems in your first book
between tasks or at the end of the day in bed
in my nightshirt sometimes tired sometimes
too awake sometimes first thing in the morning
still in bed just now I read the one about clouds
and wind and the way your mind leaps out of
control like my mind like all our minds and I
admire the way you guide me through all the leaps
the poem takes without holding my hand trusting
my instincts if not my intelligence and you do it
in one sentence without punctuation until the end
I almost wrote *the very end* but thought how
superfluous *very* is since end is end no matter
what kind and no adjective makes any difference
not even for emphasis someone is dead not
very dead not very pregnant or very divorced
as I am right now and I might have used *very*
in my own head but not out loud or in a poem
the last word in your poem is *you* meaning not
you but a woman which is what the poem's focus
finally is though we don't reach that word for many
lines yet I'm never confused in your one-sentence
poem that I'm now imitating if only to see where
it will lead if I keep it up the way I kept up my part
of my marriage even after I learned that my ex
did not he pretended to but isn't that the way
these things go when you finally relax and think
how good this is how easy to be yourself without
fuss without complaint and then the clouds you

were so grateful for in the Arkansas glare and heat
turn out to be storm clouds crouching over
the Ozarks about to devour everything in their wake
like a starving lion stalking the weakest in the herd
and along with the clouds the train sound that roar
you were warned about without time to rush
to the storm cellar the train sound after such
silence and that wind that wind but no *real* train
lifts the forest away like so many toothpicks
or rips off the roof of the carport and with it
the new car my heart felt like that and may as well
have been torn out because when that happens
you don't need it you don't want it you want to be
somewhere where you can't feel anything not even
if it's true that if you let yourself feel you will get
to the other side the fact that there is another side
to get to is hard enough to believe the way at the end
of your poem the clouds do what they want with you
you have no control the way you have no control
of the woman you want in your poem to stay
and she does not leave at least not when you wrote
the poem although that was then and this is now
isn't it?

Anniversary

Last night I set the dining room table
he's never seen. He's never seen
this apartment or the street where I live.

Or me without the thirty-five pounds
I lost after the divorce—one pound
for each of our years together.

I took out the good silver and the Wedgewood
we never used. I ate by candlelight
alone. I didn't mind. I didn't miss him.

The river light brightened as the moon rose.
I watched that. Breathed in the fruity redolence
of the chardonnay. Sipped. I ate a chicken breast

marinated in champagne and limes. I ate white rice
and fresh green beans from my neighbor's garden.
I ate alone and wanted nothing.

I didn't raise my glass. I did the one chore
that used to be his. I liked the sound
of the rinse water as I lifted the plate

from the suds, the little clink as I set it
into the dish drainer, the hum of the wine glass
as I wiped it dry. I know now where the mind

can take you when you stand by yourself
in the kitchen after a good meal.
Whatever comes next will happen anyway.

Writing Studio

You guide the thin black stream
across white sand,
stopping now and then
at something invisible, feeding
it, believing something might
actually grow there.

Soon crows arrive,
swirl down, a few at a time,
then more and more,
blackening the sand until it becomes
a field of motion, those black marks
proof there is something
alive in the field, seeds
sending their small shoots up.

People appear—some
relatives and the house
you grew up in, the woods
beyond it, the empty lot.
The voice of your father tells you
to mind your own business.
You decide to remove him,
bring in your mother instead.

Do not fool yourself.
Do not think yourself
some all-powerful god
free to invent the world

according to your whims.
You are a watcher
at the edge, a gleaner.
After the harvest is over,
you may take what you can,
but only after the crows
are done.

Overture

Portland, Oregon, February 2012

So I stepped off the streetcar
and walked to the bus stop,
marveling at the city around me,
and at the young woman I could never be
standing as if beautiful
with her tattooed neck
and metal studs through her nose and ears,
and actually she was beautiful,
singing a familiar tune, its notes of grace
filling the space between the two of us,
and suddenly too a limping man
with his cardboard WILL-WORK-FOR-FOOD sign
like the title of a poem and not his life,
but who was he then,
because he began to hum, and the woman,
teeth not yellow like his, smiling at him,
reached into the breast pocket
of her denim jacket while she sang,
and fluttered a five-dollar bill toward him
like some butterfly, which reminded me
of my mother, who sang on the bed of her death
as if song could keep her alive, or maybe
it was I who imagined this, a prayer
not for the dead but from the dying,
my mother in her purple gown
singing as if Death were not the name
of anything, but part of an overture,
her brown eyes earnest like those
of the woman at the bus stop in my new city

where I did not yet know who I would become
but now it seemed I was at least a singer
at a bus stop, for my own voice joined in
without my permission
and the three of us hovered
in the mellifluous air on the darkening sidewalk
as the bus came to us and lifted us
together and away.

Woman
in the
Painting

autumn house press, 2006

Still Life with Jonquils

The usual bowl of fruit, yes,
and at attention in a blue porcelain vase
wands of jonquils not yet bloomed,

gray-green buds
like translucent cocoons,
their wet and yellow wings

stirring against the thinning threads
of gray, about to give way—
the way a woman whose wrist

has been lightly touched beneath
the starched tablecloth recognizes
a man's invitation, its promise,

as the chatter of dinner guests blurs
into nonsense and she begins to feel
the invisible tug on the knot

fixed at the body's center
waiting
to be undone . . .

The painter knows
what not to execute, knows we bring
our own heat to the canvas,

knowing exactly how
these jonquils would look
if open.

But not letting them.

Abundance

It wasn't obvious, the way wealth glitters
from the finger or neck, the wrists.

I'm speaking of this other accumulation
inside the body,

invisible, yet we believed
we could feed on it,

though we could not see it,
could not prove it was there.

We were filled with envy, of course,
as if we were thin-haired women

and hers, thick, flowing to her waist,
her hips.

In her company we'd erase
ourselves, become her

mirror. When she smiled,
we'd smile back, when she lowered

her eyes or blushed, we'd do the same.
And when she showed us

the way a woman like her handles
serious disappointment, moving quickly

beyond it, acting as though it was the man
who had missed something,

shaking her head, pushing
her hair from her face,

her eyes nevertheless shining with forgiveness—
our eyes, too, would demonstrate

understanding, as if we too had succumbed
then been dismissed, knew

from experience what that was.
As if the man who had left her

had left us, and before that
had wanted us

the way
we had seen, had almost felt,

he had wanted her.

A Poem About Lust That's Not About Sex

I have one scar. I scraped my foot against the reef.
You know how it is when something
so startles you into your life—
you forget you're anything but eyes
or ears or mouth. It doesn't have to hurt.
I'm talking about certain swells
of music your bones recognize
as if they created them and now
they've come home. Or the first drop
of honey on the tongue. The kiss
that overtakes the body, produces
secrets you didn't know it held.

Five feet down the world changes.
Close to the reef where the sun stretches in
you can sometimes see into constricted
caves and crevices. In and out of them rush
tiny translucent fish colorful as jewels. Deeper,
blue turns black, the underside rough
and unpredictable like a man's unexpected
hand on a first date.

Some fish accumulate
in the reef's pockets, then flash all at once
as if there's an odor pulling them.
Must be like the sweetness
of dawn when I lived above a bakery.
All that yeast rising through the floor boards.

My sleeping mouth watered,
waking me. This isn't supposed to be a poem
about sex, but if I were a woman allowed
to speak her hungers, it would be.

In the Garden

Mill Cottages, Donnington, England

A squirrel fidgets at the tip of a swaying branch
and I wonder if he clings without knowing he clings.

Sometimes I remember my first time
and wonder if that girl I was held any regrets.

I think about the boy I believed I would cling to forever,
whatever I understood *forever* to mean,

no more reliable than the wind that is blind to us
and invisible.

Of course we were both young and knew
only how much we didn't know,

both of us giddy with wanting.
The squirrel leaps. The branch holds.

That's where he is now, worrying another pine cone.
I've seen this before. And him. Or one just like him.

Later there were other men
and the hopes of a young woman,

a little older now, a little more equipped,
steadying herself and more sure of her place

in her own life, not counting on
even the sturdiest looking

branch to hold her.

First Love

Between two branches of juniper
the moon appears, white sliver
in the night sky. This is to say

I haven't forgotten you.
Forgotten how you turned
from the vestibule

and never
looked back, or the way
I stood on the stoop, listless

in the failing light, and watched
as you slumped down the street,
a dark figure blending

into the wreckage of late afternoon,
no one
to anyone else. This is to say

I no longer miss you, that in fact
I haven't thought of you in years.
But I remember still the sound

of early November leaves
and the smell of them
crushed beneath the tires of some car

that pulled to the curb just as you disappeared.
Tonight's moon
will not return tomorrow. Already it climbs

beyond the branches.
This is to say, no matter
how many others I've loved,

you remain
the first flicker in that night sky—singular,
before my eyes adjusted to the darkness.

Ex

Long after I married you, I found myself
in his city and heard him call my name.
Each of us amazed, we headed to the café
we used to haunt in our days together.
We sat by a window across the paneled room
from the table that had witnessed hours
of our clipped voices and sharp silences.
Instead of coffee, my old habit in those days,
I ordered hot chocolate, your drink,
dark and dense the way you take it,
without the swirl of frothy cream I like.
He told me of his troubled marriage, his two
difficult daughters, their spiteful mother, how
she'd tricked him and turned into someone
he didn't really know. I listened and listened,
glad all over again to be rid of him, and sipped
the thick, brown sweetness slowly as I could,
licking my lips, making it last.

Ochre

I should name something so you'll know
just which yellow I mean, the ochre
of my bed shirt with the holes in one sleeve,

the ochre of the benches
at the corner of Boulevard Saint Louis, of the curtains
in the brushstrokes of Bonnard—his ochre palette,

the pallor of the woman's skin in the painting
I keep returning to. But it's not
just the color I like—

it's the sound, the way it hides in the tunnel
of the mouth without touching
anything: not the tongue that wants

to know if it tastes of syrup or salt,
not the teeth that could cut it in two
but only want to trace the shape of it,

not even the soft cheeks that seek to embrace
if only for the slightest moment
the deft word

as it enters, braces itself, hovers
like a swimmer at the edge
of a pool ready for the whistle, then escapes

into speech that dissipates before I can trap it.
So I say it sometimes—*ochre*—
just to savor the almost of it, the O

of my lips in the O of surprise
as the ochre passes through. And I spell it
the British way, *r* before *e*,

to give it that hint of unending.
So much like love it is, the way
I don't even know if it's two syllables

or one, the fickle way it simultaneously longs for
and turns away. There might be specks of ochre
in a lover's eyes, and on his neck

the faded color in the mark love left.
But always there's the delicious
pleasure that occurs as I say its name

the way I speak my lover's,
in almost a whisper, as if it were sacred—
say it, and say it, and say it again.

Woman in the Painting

Her face has disappeared. This happens
more often than you think. She sits
at a table with her hands in her lap
beside her husband, his arms
folded over one another, blue bowls
and empty glasses set out before them
and a pitcher of translucent milk.

If the woman had eyes, they would be
the hazel eyes of my mother,
her sadness exposed. If a mouth,
my mother's, her upper lip
with the scar she hid with lipstick.
Like my mother, she would be better
at listening than speaking. Afternoons
after high school my friends would come
when their boyfriends tired of them.
They would sit at a table like this one,
white and gleaming with food,
and she would listen until it was time
for my father to return, her dark hair
pulled behind her ears, her silence
laconic and wise.

Perhaps the woman in the painting
tried to speak, as my mother did,
to her father, raising her face toward him
like the mutt she once begged for,
already cowering but finally unable

to utter a sound, language transformed
to movement, to the trembling body
suppliant before him, her pupils
suddenly large and black, tears
not yet formed but forming.

The husband's face is opulent, his eyes
the color of olives at the bottom of a drink.
Perhaps the woman believes the man
she married is only her husband. For a while
that's what we all think.

Sunday Dinner

Always my grandparents arrived
disguised as harmless elders.
They'd say grace, bless the three
of us and our small residence
above my father's office.

Residence. I don't choose the word
for the poem's sake, but because
it was *their* word. I want you to hear
what I heard
through all those years

before my mother's death,
all those Sunday briskets
and pot roasts, all those potatoes
she and I peeled on Saturdays
and the pies whose crusts

we dispatched till it became ritual
the way, I thought, the making of the host
must be ritual for those who toil
in some secret bakery blessed
by a bishop. I haven't forgotten

I wrote *disguised.* And I know
you might wonder if I should have
changed that word
before I called this poem finished.
I meant

they had harmed someone.
Not me who believed
in the prayers they uttered,
but my mother
who inhabits me each time

I roll out the dough as she did,
shape it, fit it to the pan,
fill it with mincemeat or apples,
pinch the edges together
with my thumb and forefinger,

and with the tines of my fork
prick it and prick it and prick it.

Spaghetti

We stood at the stove
waiting for the water to boil.
She held it in one hand,
always the right amount
for one meal. In the other
an ache shaping itself
as she told me of the afternoon
her father had come back from work
to their ground floor apartment
her last semester of high school,
and brought the snow with him,
his feet sounding at the vestibule
like a soldier's.
But this was New Jersey, 1938,
the Great War he never went to
over, the Great Depression
not yet named.
The desk job he held for years
over too, now he said
he would not take
the only job he could get,
shoveling coal with all those
black men—*would* not,
and she would have to quit school.
She swallowed hard,
tasting it again as we stood
together in that kitchen
with its sketches of happy
farmers and their mules pulling

wagons across the wallpaper.
The pot began to gurgle,
spitting its steam. I watched
as first the dry pasta stood
at attention in the water,
then fanned out, separating,
sinking, going limp.

Nineteen-Thirty-Eight

I remember the way my mother
answered when people asked
where she'd gone to school:

South Side High, 1938,
adding the year in the same breath
though I knew

she never graduated,
yanked out
when her father lost his job.

Now it was her turn
to make herself
useful, he told her.

Hadn't he put
food on the table
all her life and all her little sister's?

How necessary
to tell a lie like hers, to answer
South Side High, 1938, and smile

without betraying
the blaze in her chest, her envy
for the questioner who likely met

her own husband at some university.
But wasn't my mother *the lucky one,*
my grandfather was fond of telling her

even into my childhood, sometimes
in front of my friends, lucky
to have got my father, a college man

who sat beside her at a ballgame
in 1939? *Just look at her*
who didn't finish high school!

Didn't I tell her then it wouldn't matter?

My Grandmother Taking Off
My Grandfather's Shoes

Every day after work he'd sit in his armchair
with its antimacassar and its plush burgundy velour
and she'd kneel on the floor to unfasten the laces,
loosen the tongues, and lift out his feet.
When I was ten I stayed for a week
and did it for her. He thought I did it
for him.

Beauty Parlor

One of the regulars had cancer
in those days before chemo,
and even after the beautician lowered
the hairdryer canister over the woman's head,

she talked nonstop about the intense heat
of cobalt treatments, the way her body burned
in places she'd rather not name,
how her skin there felt more like leather.

When she paused, the beauty parlor grew
strangely quiet: only the hum of the dryers,
the occasional whoosh of water at the sinks.
Until she spoke again, no one looked at her.

Then she droned on, but this time
about her son, who'd stopped coming by
now his wife had him
wound around her little finger.

I didn't understand yet
it wasn't his wife that kept the son away.
I was seventeen and only a guest
in this world

where my mother was a regular
on Wednesdays. That day she sat up front
among the women's magazines.
After I was done, we'd go to lunch.

And in a few days she'd tell me
her own bad news. She'd say she didn't want
to spoil my senior prom. But that afternoon
as the woman carried on and on and on,

my mother already knew what she knew.

Spark

Because each small spark must turn to darkness
in its own way, the garden snake blooms

larger from each of its skins until the one
it dies in. Upside down in the underbrush,

the turtle stills, all its tiny bones collapsed
inside its shell. The stalks of lavender

clipped from the garden for the dresser
never let go their relentless odor

that dominates still the chest
that belonged to my mother.

And my mother herself, in and out
of the hospital those last weeks,

in between
bought six new dresses, a sewing machine,

and when she couldn't sleep, studied books
of wallpaper samples.

Room 246

I hung the shopping bag
on the knob inside
the wide door of the bathroom,
draped my sweater and jeans,
even my bra, over the metal bar,
careful not to disturb
the white hospital towel
that hung there.

The dress was red and sleek,
rare for me at twenty-three,
but I wanted to be
someone else, do something
someone else might do.
Low-cut back
nearly to my waist,
scalloped neckline
almost to my breasts.
I pinched my cheeks,
bit my lips, stepped out
without my shoes
just as the night nurse
hustled in
with her packet of pills
and scowled.

But I watched
the approving eyes
of my mother instead,

her bed cranked up
so she wouldn't need
to lift her head. She
signaled with her hand
for me to spin and spin as if
it were already Saturday night
and some young man she'd never
get the chance to meet
had asked me to dance.

October 9, 1970

The same automatic doors
and the same white-haired volunteer,
the elevator and the corridor
with its antiseptic odor
and hushed voices
door after door
down one more hall and again
through the double doors—
but this morning
the lone nurse standing
before the door of 246,
and immediately inside,
the view through the window
of the other wing,
its dozens of identical windows,
and here the pale green walls
paler today behind the blank
screen of the TV
protruding from the wall
and on the movable
metal bedside table
the familiar plastic glass of water
with its bent straw
peering out like a periscope
through its plastic lid
as if only a hidden eye
had full view of the bed
and the body of the woman in it
who was once my mother.

For Weeks After the Funeral

The house felt like the opera,
the audience in their seats, hushed, ready,
but the cast not yet arrived.

And if I said anything
to try to appease the anxious air, my words
would hang alone like the single chandelier

waiting to dim the auditorium, but still
too huge, too prominent, too bright, its light
announcing only itself, bringing more

emptiness into the emptiness.

Sorrow

Sometimes it's so large
we begin to be pulled under,

so large we believe we will drown
unless the plug is pulled

and it begins to drain away
through unseen pipes that usher it

out of the sad house
and below the neglected lawn

beneath the wide street and traffic,
beyond the traffic light

and the elementary school on the other side.
Underground it slowly, steadily dissipates

into the neighborhood beyond the playground
with its innocents at recess.

For so many years I was one of them.
From the top of the slide

I could spot our beige split-level
and even its flagstone walkway.

I could sometimes make out the silhouette
of my mother retrieving letters

from our mailbox
or out on the front lawn positioning

the oscillating sprinkler.
How good her timing was then,

not leaving it in one place too long
or letting the water wet the sidewalk,

never allowing it to drown
the things she planted.

Poem in October

after Dylan Thomas

It was my twenty-third year and heaven
broke away from my reach as I stood

at her grave. Rain carved
the morning's stone face into the earth,

and the sky grayed and lowered
until they were one. Back by the trees

men smoked, as if they had nothing
better to do. But I knew as soon as I left

they would cover even
the roses my father, brother, and I

had tossed upon her as if our wishing
could do what prayer had not.

When I finally left, I thought her
gone. I am fifty-four. I was wrong.

A Simple Story

Through the kitchen window the first
red streaks of October in the sweetgum leaves,
low clouds, the monotonous street bleak
and empty of traffic, except for an occasional
truck, its grumble of gears I've grown so
used to all my years in that house I barely hear it.
At the Formica table, I envision the grandfather
I've never met: ghostlike, skeletal, his cheeks gaunt,
his blue eyes shallow with loneliness.
Why did you leave? I ask, the story my father told
all my life: his father leaving his wife and five kids
and never looking back. *Oh, that,* he says,
as if I'd handed him a penny he'd dropped
and has to stop to examine, only to find
something common and nearly worthless.

The hands of the electric clock hesitate,
then tock soundlessly. *Complicated story,*
he says, raising his coffee cup
to his mouth, sipping, putting it down.
Rain has begun, pelting, curtaining
the window glass. The room darkens,
though it is early morning. I know
he won't say anything more, though
I will wait through the storm, wait
for the sky to change, the way in real life
I sit with my ailing father at this same
table of my childhood, smiling at him,

waiting for him to speak, touching his hand
or his arm, wanting to touch his face
but not wanting to frighten or distract him
as he trembles to remember who I am.

Tiny Spider in the Bathroom Sink

I tried to be careful. It lounged along the left side
of the bowl, the smallest I've ever seen, a dot
with legs. An asterisk. I turned the water
only slightly on and aimed the thin stream
directly toward the drain and watched the spider
squat on all eight miniscule legs and raise itself again.
But after I brushed my teeth the full two minutes
to appease my dentist and held the foamy brush
under the water and flicked the bristles
with my thumb to help release the minty suds,
I forgot it was there, and opened the faucet
full force and rinsed my mouth and spat,
and saw too late the dark speck spiraling down.
And I began to understand how it happened
that after the doctor announced the bleak diagnosis
and looked down at his silent desk, my father said,
as if it were someone else whose life and death
they were discussing, *Oh, isn't that sad.*

In the Sixth Year of My Father's Illness

I wonder if he remembers the jay
that flew into the living room window

that first day he introduced himself
to the neighbor he'd known forty years.

It lay among the crushed
pine bark we spread the previous May

around the roses where the roots were smooth
and thornless, that jay so blue and *too beautiful*

to move, he said. And it stayed beautiful
even as the ants paraded in and out of its head,

removing little bits to their underground country.
Afterwards its body lay still

and still beautiful, as if death had not yet
occurred to it, its feathers

blue as the sky it once knew so well,
that sky it mistook

for the real thing. Some truths
we cannot learn. Some we forget,

as my father did, who yesterday
introduced himself to me.

Emerson Fought His

by labeling everything in his house—
its name, its use. Clock:
the thing that counts time.
Umbrella: the thing that strangers take away.

Sundays I phone my father's house
to hear his voice. *It's Andrea,* I say,
your daughter. Telephone: the thing
that says it is your daughter.

Living Room

In the cave of memory my father
crawls now, his small carbide light
fixed to his forehead, his kneepads
so worn from the journey they're barely
useful, but he adjusts them
again and again. Sometimes
he arches up, stands, reaches, measures
himself against the wayward height
of the ceiling, which in this part of the cave
is at best uneven. He often hits his head.
Other times he suddenly
stoops, winces, calls out a name,
sometimes the pet name he had
for my long-dead mother
or the name he called his own.

That's when my stepmother tries
to call him back. *Honeyman*, she says,
one hand on his cheek, the other
his shoulder, settling him
into the one chair he sometimes stays in.

There are days she discovers him
curled beneath the baby grand,
and she's learned to lie down with him.
 I am here, she says, her body caved
against this man who every day
deserts her. *Bats*, he says, or maybe,
field glasses. Perhaps he's back

in France, 1944, she doesn't know.
But soon he's up again on his knees,
shushing her, checking his headlamp,
adjusting his kneepads, and she rises
to her own knees, she doesn't know
what else to do, the two of them
explorers, one whose thinning
pin of light leads them, making
their slow way through this room
named for the living.

Exchange Student

She misses
the slowness of things, the small
room built only for tea. Pungent
steam. The certainty of it. Here

there are too many closets,
the bed is soft and high. Not
the sweet mat made of rice chaff
rolled out each night, rolled back

when the light returns. At home
doors slide away, walls disappear
into other walls, and the landscape
enters: bird, cloud, tree, mist

sifting the daylight. Here
everything seems to happen
at once. Except in the Asian wing
of the city museum the day

her host family took her,
where the white-gloved curator
unrolled the ancient scroll—
in order to see one scene

he had to roll away another.
And later how she stood
before the European still life:
a palpable plate of fruit, a slim

paring knife on the oil cloth like
the one her mother's mother used,
a single lemon, its thin peel curling
off the table and beyond the frame,

tenuous as the sloughed skin
of a garden snake. She could almost
smell the tartness of that yellow,
almost hear summer wasps

shifting into that room,
into that air she could breathe.

East Third at Ocean

Six o'clock. A few teenagers take a final swim,
shake out towels, brush sand from their bodies.
So many lost sounds, thinner than money, thinner
than a trivial thought. Behind a young boy going home

the ocean hushes. The streets, too, begin to empty,
and a few men wander into the local tavern
where it is always the same: dark mornings
become dark afternoons, and only a human voice

answers the small prayer of the woman unable
to rise from the bar. Outside
the municipal clock strikes its whole note, unnoticed,
as though an afterthought.

In separate apartments a block from the beach,
a cradle rocks, a woman's head lolls over the day's news,
a sleepy man touches his lover's cheek
with his own cheek. And in every room

sunlight narrows, retreats. In an old house closer in,
a girl's fingers rise from the keys, and yet the melody lingers.
Predictably, darkness comes
but nothing important ends because of it, nothing stops,

nothing closes. Even the wordless voice of a newborn
blends into the waning day and goes on,
mocking the way you insist
on your own significance or try to separate

mornings from afternoons, days from other days, plain years
from the years of beautiful complication—
the way you behave
as if the ocean itself were not repetitive, endless.

Rue de Lyon

Above the tall buildings, above the tabac on the corner
and the small café,
the épicerie with its outdoor
fruitstand and its burgundy awning,
and across the street, too, over the boulangerie
and the laverie and the shop that sells paper and pens,
over all the wooden double doors that mark
entrances to courtyards and apartments,
over people in their small cars and the ones
hurrying by foot on the sidewalks—above all these,
clouds thicken, they shift and spit, they darken,
and rain begins in large droplets (they could almost be counted)
then it falls in ribbons, in sheets.
Traffic dawdles, headlights flicker,
apartment shutters slam shut. And beyond the clouds,
something growls, then hurls down
its few inscrutable syllables, growls again, speaks again,
as though repetition were translation, a question the woman
huddled in one doorway could answer, as though
she might raise her face toward that unintelligible voice
and acknowledge her small place
under the canopy of one doorway where nearby
in the concrete sidewalk
the tiniest green clover has taken root
in a hole no larger than a centime
and is drenched in the downpour
and for a while longer, therefore, lives on.

Giving Birth

In time you won't even remember the pain.

— *All the books on childbirth*

On your back, heels locked in metal stirrups,
this immense volcanic shuddering
goes on against your will
as if it *were*, in fact, a volcano,
and your previous life merely a village of innocents
living on the island, used to it, barely mindful,
going about their daily repetitions, looking up
at each agitation only for a moment, thinking
it's nothing really, then returning
to their business, yanking the cord
of a lawnmower, mopping a kitchen floor,
licking stamps and sticking them one by one
onto a stack of sealed invitations.
And then again the mountain shudders.
Shudders again, this time violently.
But you are inside your breathing now, as you were taught,
and your husband's voice, his breath, that practiced duet now real,
the holding back, the pushing, the pain holding you
in its deep claws until there is nothing else.
And then the mountain erupts—you are sure of it—
erupts and erupts, its molten liquid
pushing beyond you, out, out
of your power, out, out. You wonder
where it will empty, what it will do
to those villagers who thought they had time.
Now there's no looking back, it's coming,
coming, and one of them
cries out—you hear him clearly, surely

as you heard your own pure cry moments ago,
or is this your own voice, or some part of your life
so distant it's barely attached even to memory, the way
volcanic ash showers cities hundreds of miles away,
where later the wind might shift
and a young man rising
onto the street from the metro,
brushes a bit of soot from his face.

Remission

The grass hums with its bees and its mowers,
a breeze rises,

and leaves you would not have seen yesterday
lift and settle, lift and wander

a few at a time, yard to yard. Today
you wander, too, away from the house,

the neighborhood, along the road and up
through the pin oaks and pines that cover the hill.

In the hollow on the other side you stop
among the apple trees now empty

except for a few small fruits too high for anyone's reach.
You have never been this rich.

You lie on the rare ground, that small truth you had
somehow not counted on, sweet

with the wine of fallen apples,
empty and sweet yourself, nearly drunk

on the sound of your own breath
rising in its bounty from your mouth.

The Other Life

story line press, 2001

One's real life is so often the life that one does not lead.

OSCAR WILDE

One less hope becomes
One more song.

ANNA AKHMATOVA

Those Summer Sundays

Sundays my father would join us
at the club pool, his skin
white and delicate as cigarette paper

on the one day he took
from the women who lined
his waiting room

month after month.
I waited at the shallow end.
He rose from the board

and dropped
straight as a table knife
without a splash. Always

the women stared, women
from whose bodies he had pulled
daughters, released sons.

And never
would he surface
until he had maneuvered through the depths

to the place where I stood. Giddy, I would close
my eyes as he hoisted me
from the flawless water

on his shoulders, the two of us
one thing, perfect and tall.
I did not know then

of the sometimes dangerous
entrances of men, how some will lift
what others slowly drown.

Goodness

As my husband set the table for breakfast,
I stood at the kitchen counter in my pink chenille bathrobe,
its pockets worn through, waiting for the toast to rise,

and realized that this, too, I would lose—
this moment so routine
it would soon disappear into the daily machine of our lives

like the beautiful pebble I dropped on the beach
and moments later couldn't find.
As good as it was to be home in this good house

with my husband humming something familiar,
the tea already steeping, the juice poured, even the butter
waiting in its porcelain plate on the table,

there was nothing I would remember it by, and I knew it.
If the phone had rung with bad news about my father
even the way the sun angled onto the rug would have brought

the bad news back again each time,
and I could never have worn that bathrobe again.
Is this why Anne Frank's diary matters?

At another place, another time,
the life of a thirteen-year-old girl would have disappeared
into a box in the upstairs closet,

a few pages of it read, perhaps, by her grown-up son, and then
because he had to drive his daughter to school
and pick up the paper on the way, he would have closed it,

promising himself to someday read the rest, then whistled
down the stairs in his herringbone vest and jacket
to where his daughter waited in the sunlit hall.

Love Song Ending with
a Line by Horace

What the eye sees
with its magic attachments
when you look at him
and he looks back

What the ear hears
when its words are not words at all
but the wild birds
of another's heart

What the mouth knows
but cannot speak

What the cheek feels
when the lashes of his eyes
play upon it
a secret music

When the limbs sigh
as the body lies
anticipating

And the mouth knows
but cannot speak

And the hands—
the hands that want
everything

for themselves
and won't be spared
and won't be told
to stop

And the mouth knows
but will not speak

What the heart has had
no fingers of any hand
will hold

Why I Married Him

In front of the whole class
when I stopped mid-sentence, lost
for a single word, silence
pushing its way in, unstoppable
as a wave, my mind like a sunbather
weary from the heat of the beach, asleep
in the constant glare, the sea's drone
masking the sea's approach,
waves moving imperceptibly closer,
about to take over,

he found it, the lifeguard who had sat quietly
all summer long, more looked at
than looking, found and shoved
the right word into the right place
like a wall built to keep the sea out,
and saved me.

And I knew that with him life would be
like that. Even on the calmest days
he'd stay up on his ten-foot chair
watching, ready to hold
even the ocean back.

Poem Written at Home
While You Fly Over the Atlantic

When you were small I'd try
to wake you without being heard—a breeze
barely disturbing your hair, a bit of sunlight

on your shoulder. I wanted you to assume
you had stirred on your own,
that I had appeared

by a kind of ordinary magic. Or
sung you to sleep
and stayed.

Today I look out at these trees
and imagine the sky
looks down upon them

as a mother would
with their seasonal changes
it anticipates and prepares for.

It is merely backdrop, after all,
even with its two bodies
which illuminate everything.

From the airplane window
you look out now at the blackness
you can't touch, yet which holds you

in its perfect, invisible arms
and will deliver you
onto this earth (I must believe)

as I once did, watching you emerge
out of my singular body
whole and alive and on your way

for the first time
someplace important
without me.

Hunters

Dressed in their green spotted drabs to blend in
with trees, my brother and his new friends, then
nineteen, erected their dark tents and dug
a latrine, then gathered twigs from the edge
of their camp and the driest leaves, and at
twilight all of them assembled, then bent
their heads for a moment over their Tang
or their coffee or tea, and one boy sang
a little prayer in the unarmed quiet
(at night sometimes my brother still sings it),
and even the air began to settle
except for the occasional rattle
of insects and in the nearby distance
mortar fire from Da Nang, insistent.

Wound

When you asked if I wanted to see
and I said yes, you opened your robe,
lifted off the gauze, and exposed
a barbed wire fence cut
through a field of snow.
The snow wasn't white exactly
but used or forgotten, the air
hardened by winter so that
to breathe was to choke.
And along its black length
that separated into two
your past and your future,
that fence was streaked
with indecipherable detritus
as though some small animal
had been dragged from its life into it
and died there, its clots of fur
still frozen in the barb.
This is your chest, I told myself,
not some deserted pasture
flattened by winter over
what is lost or missing.
I should have closed my eyes
or pictured the ocean instead.
Twenty-seven years after your death
I still can't turn away. I shut my eyes
and see your chest stitched closed.
If only poems were the only places
to know such cold.

Reading Aloud to My Mother

After dinner on those last days
we hoped would linger

until the thinning moon rose
into the numb sky,

I sat beside her bed
and read from the novel she'd begun

months before on her own.
At first the words wouldn't leave

the page. Then, like crows
nibbling invisible debris

on the uneven horizon long enough
to grow invisible themselves,

they unpredictably
lifted all at once above it

and pushed across the darkening sky,
a tribe of inky letters

on a page that itself was slowly growing black
until the words, there or not, were mute

as the new moon that in a few days
would rise and fall again in the black sky

and I would be there and watching
and would not see it.

A Tree Like This One

Once, when my mother was alive
and the Russian olive tree in the backyard not yet
blown over by the storm, and we lay awhile

under it on a blanket, feeling lazy, looking
up into the gray of its leaves,
teasing one another

not at all like mother and daughter
but two friends who had poked
pins into their index fingers and had sworn

by the blood, we decided to pretend
that, like her grandparents, we had walked
all night through a forest to get there

and taken everything important
with us, everything
we could carry, that is,

having buried the copper pots
and taken the Seder dish,
but thinking, too,

that her grandparents would have walked
out under a tree just like this one, pretending
they had already arrived

in the New World, that this
was only a picnic, after all,
here on the uneven grass

that a little way off they could hear
my mother and me
already alive and giggling.

How He Warmed Himself

All night the wind railed in the trees.
Their father closed the windows tightly as he could
against the noise, and, assured they were asleep, crunched out,

quietly as possible, into the snow-packed world,
too soon for shoveling, too late
for anything else.

He must have thought himself invisible
in that white world
or small and doomed

beneath his own canopy of breath
that must have somehow seemed
a separate thing.

As he lifted the garage door and clunked it down again
against the muffled light, and slipped
the key into the ignition, and turned it,

he must have thought past them,
past the photographs arranged chronologically on the hallway wall
and all their pastels on the refrigerator,

past the summer days that grew lazily green on the other side
of the world he could not reach, or wait for.
He must have settled in and warmed himself

against the winter storm stacking its white cache against one side
of the house, his own chronic storm
waning inside him,

against the furniture they still owed money on
and the car itself, against his unheld rage
that rested now like a shriveled thread on the dashboard.

He must have warmed himself
against the lingering bit of restlessness or second thoughts,
and the blackness they knew nothing of

that crowded in, against even
these words he couldn't guess he'd cause,
and all the other wordless deeds

the dead give birth to.

My Father's Sweater

It was snug on him anyway, she said,
his wife, my stepmother, when she offered it
like a monthly magazine already read,

nothing she would miss if I took it,
something to keep me
warm in the bitter afternoon of late

March, to turn my thoughts from the empty bed
where she said he had lain for a week.
She hadn't phoned. She kept

believing he'd recover, that he'd guide her
down the hospital corridor
to their car as he'd done before,

my sleek father who'd kept slipping
into childhood, my brilliant daddy with only
saliva on his tongue.

How the worn wool glowed, how its burgundy twill
warmed me as if it were the wine
of the same name and I had had my fill.

I folded the sleeves at the wrists, pushed them up like
small accordions.
All the way home on the plane, I lay back

in my window seat surrounded
by the sad comfort of his familiar redolence.
Ten years later I'm astounded

I never wore it again. Not once have I lifted it
from the closet shelf where it lies
in the pungence of cedar, out of sight

like the soldier my father had been
in the forests of Germany, the charred
chateaux of France, where he had hidden

his fear like a stolen radio, its voices foreign
but alive, indecipherable and distant
as now his own voice has grown,

inscrutable as faith,
insistent
as the long absence of his breath.

The Other Life

The life you wish you had lived
inhabits the lavender scarf
you lift now and then

from the dresser drawer.
Like perfume, it invades
every room in your house

with possibilities
until your body is filled—
that body

anyone can touch.
It holds on tight
the way on an autumn afternoon

the fig tree loses
only its leaves and not
the fruits that have turned

in on themselves
like tiny fists.
Must you give up

this life, whose doors
you have dreamed open?
Though you have parted

its curtains, worn
its moonlit glow?
Haven't you earned

this grief that makes you
unable to breathe
anything else?

These are the days you linger
at the dinner table eating
nothing, the other life

wanting you only
to want it,
to keep it known,

an initialed handkerchief
without an owner.
It is palpable

as that tiny mahogany chest
made to hold letters
you wish you'd received,

or that diary whose empty pages
have already yellowed.
Or your heart which beats

only in the other life, the life
you covet and protect,
the one you invent and invent

because it invents you back.

Longing

Every word I write is made of it.
A small boat of popsicle sticks saved all summer

and glued together by a child
is stuck in the rushes.

There are woods in which I have never walked
and perfume in those woods.

Even if I could go there
I wouldn't be able to find its source.

I say this: if words could be laid down,
if they could be held,

my longing would end.
But words are not what they say.

They echo only the sound
of a voice, a remnant, itself

an echo. They sting
and disappear like the beautiful

hornet whose nest is nearby—
that quick, that painful.

Some words undo me—your name,
for example, or the words you write. You

who are both lifeboat and line,
if you were here now

I would touch
and touch you and never have enough.

If the rushes let go, that boat will break up
and travel unrecognizable

stick by stick in the tide.

Afterwards

Shy, she leans away from him and sighs, thinks
the way the neon sign blinks off and on
through the curtains—gold and blue, gold and blue—
is a sign of something larger than themselves.

He fiddles with her hair, gets up the nerve
to hum a tune he knows she likes, endures
her unresponsive back, observes
the curtains changing colors with the lights.

Talking in bed ought to be easiest—
but silence, that untameable weed, thick
and uncrushable as passion, flourishes between
them now, numb at the mattress's separate edges,

her prom dress upright and stiff in the corner
standing on its layers of crinolines
as though she ordered it there, as though
the girl who had danced in it hours before had not yet left,

as though his tux folded on the chair and the pair
of cuff links side by side on the table meant business,
as though, after all, it wasn't their bodies that mattered
nor the months the two of them had planned this hour.

What words could she use to erase all this and return
to the night before when she modeled for her father
showing him where her corsage would go and where
tomorrow she would pin the boutonnière?

The Other Side of the Story

"When you reach my age, you begin to remember
the truth of things."

Esther Hollander, age 91

Ever since I could tell it, I've told this side
even to myself, the one that could have been

photographed, frame by frame. In which he carried me
through the doorway and onto the bed, in which

though the fire blazed, the heat in the room was something
the two of us created, never mind it was November,

the shutters on the windows frozen shut, never mind
we were practically children, both nineteen.

I've told the story so many times I thought I'd forget
the other side, blurred for years in my private mirror,

though now the glass has cleared, and I see precisely
how cold it was that first time in the cabin on the lake,

and how long he took to build the fire.
That it went out quickly, that he tried a few more times,

then let it die. I saw that he was clumsy.
Without his shirt his chest was pale, his arms thin.

How much it hurt when he entered. And after he'd fallen asleep,
how I stared at my skirt and blouse

folded over the back of the chair, and the logs
barely charred in the open fireplace. I see that room

so clearly now, how small and barren it was
and how insignificant.

What the Married Man Dreamed

Though he sensed he was only dreaming,
he lay back on the bed, watched her unpack,

watched as she turned and grappled
with the fact of his being there. Whether or not

she knew she was someone he'd only invented
for the night, someone he needed finally in a room

like this, motel or not, she moved toward him,
lay down beside his body, touched his face.

That was all there was, all there had to be.
Dream or not, it was something to keep,

the way her electricity spread
through him, under them the bed

fully made, all their clothes on, her skirt
not even lifted, and, except his heart,

nothing in his life disturbed.

Part of the Story

"Just leaning toward someone is part of the story."

William Stafford

Though she may not even remember
the way his arm felt pressed against hers,

he remembers. In bed with his wife sometimes
he imagines her body instead. He says her name

only to point out how plain she is, how bored
she'd make the unlucky man who had to

endure her. Weekdays he drives the routine
streets to work. He brushes by her desk, borrows

a paper clip, a stack of envelopes. He thinks
how safe this is. Leaning toward someone

is only part of the story, the way his arm felt
pressed against hers, the center.

Delta Flight 1152

After the first drink, you can be
what you're not. It's so easy, all you must do

is answer this man's questions with truths
you've just invented—*on my way to the annual meeting*

of master magicians, or to a conference of physicists
or international bankers—and your life is enviable,

new. Tell him you're sad because you're on your way
to your sister's wedding and you're in love

with her fiancé. Wipe your eyes,
sigh, mention almost under your breath the baby

you had to give up, the job. You're the one
who introduced them, you couldn't stop yourself, he would come

to your desk at the office. How lonely he was,
how young. But if you reveal the afternoon

of lunch on the rooftop, how for you
it wasn't enough, there's certain danger

this man, his drink finished, ice diluted
in the bottom of his plastic cup, will lean too far

into your invented life. He'll offer his handkerchief.
You'll finger his embroidered initials. He'll touch your arm,

hand you his card. His voice unsteady,
he'll tell you to call him at home—you,

an only child on her way
to see the ocean for the first time. You, who have managed

to live a moral life, whose troubled heart has never
surrendered, now with your wild and dangerous

lies, you could turn toward this stranger
and open.

On the Other Side of the World

He was dancing again
with the other man's wife, while her husband dozed

in the boozy room. The music moaned from its little box
in the corner. The dancers swayed a little closer.

We were all tipsy. In the kitchen women giggled.
The odor of coffee rose.

I sat on the couch tired of trying to chat
in a language I didn't own,

making over and over
the same mistakes. The music faded, his hand

now on the small of her back, hers
on the back of his neck, their feet

barely moving, the weight of what would come next
shifting right, then left.

And where were you, my love? I stood at the window
on the other side of the world

and observed the predictable
moon, that ravaged, over-used philanderer's tool.

Like me, it kept its place, barely visible
in the otherwise unmarked heavens.

An Explanation

"Frank was missing something, and women would do anything to find out what it was."

James Salter

It's nothing, really, just a kind of trick I use
to keep them. I look up from their bodies

with a tenderness I've maintained after we've made love
wishing to extend even further

that welcome moment of grace that settles in
just after the inevitable diminishment

over which neither of us has any control.
I look up from their bodies and glance

toward a window, if there is a window,
or a closet door or a calendar on the wall, perhaps

a candle on the bedside table with its rarefied flame.
If there's a painting above the bed, I make sure it's safe

before we even begin to undress or lie down
to undress one another. Once

it was one of those portraits of Jesus
naked and bleeding, which ruined everything.

I'm all there when I'm there. Yet sometimes, I've learned,
it's better to lift them out of themselves by giving

a little bit less. I don't mean to be cruel,
cutting them off from my pure attention. I only want

the deepest they'll give me, the thing you can't ask for—
they don't know where it is themselves. I think

of Valentino who was forced to use only his eyes to speak
and his body, the sound of his voice kept irretrievably

from us, that incomplete circle that wanted finishing,
and we, of course, supplied the best.

That's it, really. Leaving something necessary
out that they'll fill in. Something small, of course,

but important, something at first you don't withhold
so they'll notice right away when you do.

Remember the page in the children's magazine
that displayed a kitchen or a yard and asked you to find

the ten things wrong? An upside-down
clock, say, or a dog in a tree?

It's taken me years to learn this, and it works.
A woman will nest herself for as long as I want her.

She gives me more and more of everything, tries
to fill my gaps, plug holes in my conversation.

When she finally tires of her own failures, and leaves,
it never hurts. I always have at least her sympathies

and her longing. There are so many beautiful women
lighting this world. It's the only way I've found

to possess them.

Woman and Husband

The fray between us over, spilled and mopped,
this bed a shoreline finally reached, he stops
explaining, stops my mouth as well, and with
his chest against my back, his breath
familiar in my hair, insists
on silence. The clock is all we hear: it ticks,
we breathe. The hickory near our window
vibrates gold, our door is closed,
the sun ignites the clock. Is it enough
to turn and kiss his mouth?
Or will I feed on air that someone else
has breathed? Or taste what she spit out? Enough.
When I first conceived him in my life
I craved the softness of his voice, his eyes
that penetrated mine. Disease
is made of less.
How soon the sun will leave the clock, the trees
brush grayish tremblings on the chest of drawers.
His breath is heavy at the hollow of my neck.
What mercifulness this is. A gift—
a broken gift
I'm finally willing to give back.

What I Need It For

I meant it for my desk, to hold my pencils and pens,
but I need flowers instead, yellow-centered
summer daisies to bluster into my poems.

Each morning when I trudge into my study,
rain or shine, rain or (mostly) more rain,
one look at these white pinwheels

each with its own little sun, and I can begin
to believe my own weather is different.
But what if you stepped into that room

just now, awkward as our first day, hesitant
and wordless? The flowers could have been
roses, of course. Better they aren't. Better

they are common flowers, the kind
you plant only once,
and year after year they return.

Confessional Poet

Sometimes when I read my poems
I think only about the dinner to come,

about the chardonnay and the gaze
of my host, the way he will study me

across the table's white ironed cloth
and tapered candle, and the way

I'll consider his mouth, his lips. So,
I apologize. I confess. As you listen,

I may be someplace else, though my voice
does the work you expect, my mouth

rounded over the words they express,
my lips poised at the edge

of my muted consonants, my suitable vowels.
And though we are together

in this small auditorium or lecture hall or
classroom or café, already I have betrayed you

as easily as I used to betray
the congregation at church. At sixteen

I would open my mouth to sing
all those solemn hymns to Jesus

as I clocked in at the job
of making my face do one thing,

my mind another. I portrayed
one of the earnest,

my pure face invoking the presumption
of sinlessness, the countenance

of belief. But while I sang
I conjured the minister

without his robes,
sidling up behind me, pressing

his nonsectarian body against mine.
Oh, I was a sinner,

at least in thought—the same thing
according to my Catholic friends.

Now I stand at a lectern and confess
everything—the lies I have lived or invented,

the truths I have hidden in them.
I describe in detail the delicate

fruits of the forbidden and all the ways
I have enjoyed them—

the fruits themselves and the telling,
that other way to taste them again.

Fellow sinners, as I mouth these words
I want you to believe,

I am imagining another place
I've never been, another lover

I will bring to life, another journey
on which I could take you, another trip

on which I will never otherwise go.

How It Is Done

You go inside, take off your shoes,
enter the room everyone else believes is too dark,
open the small drawer of the ebony desk
your father brought back from his year in Japan
with its carved heads and torsos of dragons and serpents—
so many your mother sent it to the cellar.
You take out the pen and the bottle
of India ink, black as the dragons' ebony eyes,
then from the back the sheaf of paper, so white
it is new snow against the window the day
the power lines were downed by the storm.
For a long time you look through that window,
and finally make your way out of that room,
that house. You walk without considering the hidden
existence of sidewalks or the carless streets. You are careless.
You tunnel through drifts or climb them,
and you keep on like this until it snows enough
to hide your way back, as you are doing now,
one word at a time.

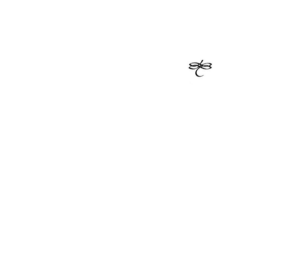

House
Without
a Dreamer

story line press, 1993

When She Named Fire

it was a sound
she uttered, not a considered thing, nothing
her mind did. It was a sound
that burned her throat to come out
and announce itself for the thing
burning outside her
where the trees had been down
for years. It lit the sky
then disappeared and changed
to something black.

When she named the sun, she didn't think
of fire at all. *Sun,* she claimed,
because it was huge and unexplainable,
a oneness that she loved
for its ability to command
the whole sky and the earth, too—
and because it was the warmest thing
she knew, and she sang
its tunes and missed it every night.

She didn't name the moon at all.
That was the name it gave itself.
At night she heard it call. To her
it was another kind of sun, still white
but cold, an icy light
that narrows as it grows, that is not
light at all.

She thought she gave love's name
to love, that beating thing she could not
still. She might have called it
bird. Or *fire* again
for fire inside that gives no light
but burns and burns and does not
stop until she touches
what she loves, and then it only burns
again and makes her want
to name it something more.

The Color of the Sky

No matter what I tell you about the sky tonight,
even if I tell you everything I know
about its dark rich blue, faded here
and there like the velvet jacket my mother
used to wear, and how much I loved her
when she wore it, how much I loved to touch
her arm or think about touching it, how sometimes
I would even walk deep into the walk-in closet,
dark as the sky is tonight, and reach
and find it by touch, and know it, electrically,
the way I know your body in our bed at night,
in the black room of that room, way in the back
where no one could find me, in the blue-black
night of that soft cave, and the smell of it,
the faded smell of my mother there and the way
I felt—all velvet and alone and blue myself,
and somehow safe, just safe. No matter what I tell you
about the color of the sky tonight, you will not know
enough about the sky at all, about its magnificent blue
that I know I could touch, that changes and disappears
no matter how much I say, no matter how much
I want it to stay.

Beginning and Ending with Lines
from Shakespeare

Whoever made us believe that all the world's a stage
must have known we'd drive as slowly as the car would go
past the aftermath of the accident, one young man holding
another man's head above the reddened pavement,

a woman still in the passenger seat holding her shoulder,
another, her hair in pink plastic curlers, pacing
that brief space between the cars, her eyes crazy,
her little boy in her arms, her girl trying to slow her

down. Whoever made us believe must have known
we would save that scene, however brief, save
even the sky's cumulus relief of gray against gray against gray,
that, against our wills, we'd take it all home

and play it again when we were most alone,
waiting by a telephone in a hallway,
praying him home, praying that other day's images away,
not wanting to see anymore the quick white bone

jutting through the man's leg as he lay
with his head in the other man's arms, not wanting, over and over,
to hear that ambulance racing to save not only
him. We believe we are more important than they,

that this cannot really happen to us. This is a game, we insist,
the next car we hear will be his pulling in,
this is only a stage
and all the men and women merely players.

Pigs

It is not the wolf
but his howl in the hollow wind

they fear. His mouth is a great cave
and that howl the master of it—

that sound calling like the night,
calling what is dark to its vacant center.

Straw by straw, stick by stick,
brick by solid brick, there is no way

to keep that sound from entering.
But try. Move in together, give birth,

have other kinds of dreams. Sleep
with a light turned on, with cotton in your ears.

And by the evening fire tell the stories
of your ancestors. Tell how clever they were,

how they tempted the devil from the skins
of the innocent. How they burned him

from those useless lives: Catholics, Jews,
witches, saints. And with fire like this.

With fire like this.

Fire

The house was not touched.
But the trees are charred, our yard
is black, the grasses bladeless.
Everything we own looks different
now. Even knickknacks seem to have more
weight, the walls have grown, the furniture
replaced with replicas. And our son

does not want to go to bed.
"What if it happens again
in my sleep," he does not ask,
but says. I sleep

much lighter now myself.
Weeks later I am up at 3 a.m.
to look at him, his face so perfect
in the moonlight. There's so little we can
count on. He's nearly nine. He nearly died
when he was born. And now we've come
this far. I see he's got the corner
of the blanket in his fist.
I want just this: to watch him
breathe all night, learn everything,
everything he is.

Weeds

The last time I saw my mother
alive, I remember driving the familiar
miles to the hospital, sensing that this
might be the last time, and suddenly seeing
everything as if I'd never see it again:
houses, yards, fences, trees, weeds that grew
along the edge of one driveway where
I waited for a light. It had been weeks
this time, and now she'd stopped eating.
There were dandelions on the hospital grounds
and crabgrass and pigweed. I remembered
the necklace she showed me how to make once
from dandelion flowers. The clouds made
shadows on the walkway. The elevator
smelled like medicine and powder.
In the bed my mother slept. Her breath
was uneven, and I wondered if she dreamed.
The room was filled with greenhouse
flowers. I wore that necklace for hours,
until it grew too limp to keep.

Choice

Whatever the truth is, I remember it
this way: the two of them arguing
over a dress, which one would be
the *right* dress, Ruth insisting
the flowered one my mother'd worn
to parties, Helen, whose face
by now was dark, her voice nasty,
accusing any choice that wasn't black
of blasphemy, disgusted anyone would even
think *that* dress. And then they looked
to me, her only daughter, after all, now
twenty-three and older than I'd ever be
again, and wanted me to arbitrate.
I'd be a traitor, whatever I said.
So I looked at them a long while,
nothing in my head but the picture
of my mother's face that morning
with finally a little peace in it again,
her body in the hospital bed,
the last bed, the last
face she'd ever have
for me. What did it matter
what they would dress her in
tomorrow, that day that only I
would always see? *Naked,* I thought
the way she came. And then
I turned from the darkness
and the flowers, which were

the same, and from the two
of them in their overwhelming
grief, which had taken them to this
tiniest of places, and what I thought
I said.

Grief

"The most terrible part of a great sorrow is not
the beginning, when the shock of grief throws one
into a state of exultation which is almost anaes-
thetic in its effects, but afterwards, long afterwards,
when people say, 'Oh she has gotten over it.'"

Isadora Duncan

It is the cave you visit
in your dream—no
stars, no moon, so
you swim naked, knowing
you cannot be seen.
You move down, down
through the black water,
and there is no end.
You see nothing, feel
only small waves passing
through your ears
as you descend.
It is not different
from other caves
in other dreams:
a secret place,
and you have learned
to breathe in it.

When You Hear His Name

unexpectedly,
long after you have claimed

it wouldn't mean anything, you know
you have found the one name

you can never say,
never even bear to hear

even if it is now someone else's name,
a neighbor's child

and his mother snapping it at him
like a whip.

You try to make that sound just
a white sheet

the wind slaps
on the taut line. But you become

that line
holding everything above

the earth, stretched
house to post and back

again to house. Or you are
the post, placed

only to hold
the laundry up, keep

the line straight. You are not
the house, not a thing

someone can enter.

Women at Fifty

after Donald Justice

All their doors
have closed and their daughters'
rooms betray a familiar faint perfume
that says *I'll not be back.*

They pause sometimes
at the top of the stairs
to stroke the banister,
its perfect knots.

They invite other women now
only to clean. And like queens in fairy tales
they turn their heads from mirrors
that hold secrets they've kept

even from themselves,
as they look into their husbands' faces
when their husbands say
they only look.

Women at fifty
corner a cricket with a broom
and do not kill it, but shoo it out of the house
into the abundant silence.

Soup

At 4 p.m., while her ex is sitting
in his easy chair somewhere in the gray
of his Iowa landscape, his desk high

with obligations, the unread
Sunday papers piled by his feet,
the winds faint, the traffic fainter,

the snowless cold out every
window of his house, and light
thrown through the clouds in such a way

there is no doubt what time
or day or state this is,
a little farther south

she will be standing at the kitchen sink
of her too familiar house, scraping
vegetables for soup and looking

out at the same bleak sky, trying
to remember how brilliant
the brittle trees have been,

listening to their fits
and twists in the wind, paring
carrot peels into the sink, then potato,

letting them pile there like spent
snake skins. If only he
would open this door, how warm

the afternoon would feel, how different
the falling of the light, how autumn,
not winter, the soup.

Therapy

for James Twiggs

Years back when I thought
I needed that kind of listener,
I paid a therapist enough
to call her mine and sat
in her velvet chair an hour
each time and watched
that hour die and watched
her face and through her
window just behind I watched
the haze of Boston's sky
which was so alive
I thought it watched me back
as I spoke my mind
and it pulled clouds
across her frame from gray
to darker gray.

That kind of hour is like
a dream. And even now
I keep remembering
more the way she seemed
so like a cat
stretching, purring, preening
as she sat with her shoes
off and her legs curled up
and sometimes touched her
mouth and sometimes scratched
her brow. I remember that
more than anything she did

or did not say. She did not
save me. She may have
tried. I was lost
to time and men and, in my twenties
then, I kept mistaking time alone
for emptiness. And then one day
she fell asleep and even snored,
my voice a drone, the sky a storm.
Insulted, scared, cured? I guessed
that that was that. I tiptoed out
and took the streetcar home
and got a cat.

Firmly Married

is what he said but as he said it
swayed a little in my direction,
the hair on his neck so like
my son's, barely there, but golden
if you bothered looking.

He was looking at me anyway
no matter what he said,
a benefit of having spoken
his excuses so I'd excuse
anything he did thereafter.

I walked away.

And afterwards I thought
how easily he'd escaped
whatever I may have taken
from that look, that he wanted it
to be *my* invention, the way

I used to pull my stockings up
pretending not to notice Richie
watching, when I was nineteen
and wanted secretly my first time
to happen already, but wanted it

to be *his* doing, this undoing
I longed for desperately,
the way this man wants
some blameless ruin.

Permission

When you have stood at the door
longer than two friends ought to,
one of your mates upstairs
tucking children in, the other
out of town; and when you stand
not gazing off into any distance
at all, recognizing that there
isn't any distance that wants
attention, except the three or four
inches between your face and his,
that that is the distance you'd like
permission to disclaim, erase, void,
you stop.

You step back, find something
simple and unnecessary to do
with your hands, hoping you won't
touch his arm or his face, hoping
he won't move any closer,
that he'll discover something
in the way, something that will
sway him somewhere else. Or you hope
words will come, right words
that will shape what is necessary
to shape, so you can keep this
the way you want it: the wanting
and the stepping back. Not the finishing,
not that. As though the *right* words,
if you could find and say them, could really

save you, save you from saying what is
not right, like *yes* or *yes* or especially
the *yes* that is not spoken, which—with
or without permission—you seem already
to be saying nonetheless.

Black

Before his wife came back
she rose from his bed into the black
dress she'd brought, so stark a color
for early autumn, and buttoned it
all the way to her neck and said goodbye
and drove toward home. All day along that road

as she grew warm, she unbuttoned buttons one by one.
What little she has known of passion. It takes in
everything, seduces the most innocent.
Only road kill seemed to own that road: skunk, skunk,
armadillo, possum, possum, possum. Passion

travels in the dark—the animal
we do not truly know, the one
we never pet, the one so foreign
to our lives we do not have a sense
of what it eats or where it sleeps, and only know
its death. She meant

to watch the hills instead, the greens
reduced, the reds so dominant
the rest pull back.
Her mother told her don't wear black until
you're grown. Back then she thought
of widow's clothes. The kind

of passion she has known
at first is wet and thunderous and new as grass

that's greener after rain, then briefly blazes red,
then is black and thunderous and wet—and then
the nakedness, the nakedness again.

No One Wants to Be the Witch

no matter which story
this is. But today
in this story I'll play

the dark one, try on
her difficult clothing
that dazzles yet so easily

slips away. I'll sit
in the clearing and wait
for the boy to come with his simple

hunger and his single trick. If it's his tongue
he wishes to satisfy, I'll conjure the cinnamon
house. If it's love,

that chivalric game of bluff we play
to feed the animal the kind of power
it needs, I'll stay up

in the tower, fool him with my lonesome
melody and my long untangling. If it's fear
he wants, I'll give him thorny

messages to cut through and a little
blood. No matter who
I truly am, sorrow-filled

human, loneliest woman in love
only with him, I'll give him whatever
he's after, whatever he believes

he needs to see, be it princess
or virgin, whimpering
animal or mute, whatever

helplessness wants rescuing
and he both hero
and sword. But what will make him call me

witch, in the end, is how much of this
he will conjure for himself, how he will someday
know lust for what it was, love

for what it might or never
could have been. He'll be his own
witch then.

Snow White

It was actually one of the dwarfs
who kissed her—Bashful,
who still won't admit it.
That is why she remained in the forest
with all of them and made up
the story of the prince. Otherwise,
wouldn't you be out there now
scavenging through wildflowers,
mistaking the footprints of your own
children for those little men?
And if you found some wild apples
growing in the thickest part, if no one
were looking, wouldn't you
take a bite? And pray
some kind of magic sleep
would snatch you
from the plainness
of your life?

Getting Back

Thirteen days away, then three different planes
and the airport lounges between them,
the three hours north in the car
watching the white line blur toward home,
all the time wanting to see only
your eyes instead of the lights
of oncoming cars, wanting
your body back and the deep forgiving step
into that dark lake where we swim
toward the darkest part
waiting for light.
Wanting nothing else, taking
only what we believe we have to have
and finally reaching that limbo place
of not wanting, the wanting itself—
a plane so huge, so heavy you cannot believe
it will ever rise—having lifted with grace
and impossible ease.

This Will Be My Only

unfaithfulness.
I will take the man
you used to be
and remember him.
I will draw his lines
on your hands at night
while we lie awake
and speak to him
in dark places, even
while you sleep.
He will not leave me.
His turns will not be digressions,
nor will he place new feet on the sill
each day when he enters.
And his words will be few,
but I will know them the way
any woman knows the body
of her lover. I will hear them
every time we touch.

What I Will Be When
I Cannot Be with You

When the leaf turns
but does not fall, that will be me.
And when the leaf finally falls,
even if you are looking instead
at a flower, that, too, will be me.
And if the flower blooms, huge
and reckless, the soft yellow powder
inside that comes off on the legs
of a bee or on your finger or stains
the tip of your nose will be me,
as will the bud's seed that no one
sees when the bud fails to open,
and the vacant spot on the tree
that you see when you look again
and the leaf has dropped.

What I Want

When I've had enough of silence,
enough of its fog so thick this single
headlight I've become
beams out alone
into its soupy darkness,
suddenly I know
how lost I am.

This is the way
that longing always goes.
A stubborn light is shot in one
direction and does not go out, is not
returned. I want

to change this longing if I can.
I want to stop discounting
what I am. I want whatever's out there—
perhaps a word, perhaps a man—to part
that silence,

to clear the road ahead,
to signal dogs and rabbits,
to warn oncoming traffic
that someone mean and tired of longing
is speeding down this forlorn
road, careening fast past everything
she knows, top down,
radio blaring, leaning hard
on her persistent horn.

Poem for My Brother, Manager of a Go-go Bar in Roselle Park, New Jersey

Some night between midnight and three
when the last of the great pinchers
has finished his final drink
and you have taken his keys
and walked him out to the slick
New Jersey street, wet with the glaze
of approaching morning, and told him
to sleep it off in his own back seat,
then walked slowly back to the bar,
picking up debris and trash, tidying
the sidewalk, thinking about tomorrow,
about the girls who don't mean anything
or the greasy spot on the pavement
that is always there, no matter what
the weather, the streetlight out front
the only moon you ever see—
before you step inside and tend
the last of the sweeping and breathe
the last of the evening's smoke,
the music turned down but still on
so you won't be lonely, it would be sweet
if you would remember me, your only sister
ten years older and distant in miles
and habit, living for fifteen years
in the backwoods of a southern state
you've never seen, in a dry county
(where there still are such things),
rubbing the backs of her achy legs

with alcohol to suffocate
the chiggers, as she sits at the edge
of her homemade deck facing east
and thinks of you, as someone might
leaf through a history book and glance
at the pictures of places she has been,
or bends over a child's telescope
taking turns with her son and husband,
and names planets at a glimpse.
Tonight the music here is calm as crickets
and in a minute it is all I'll hear
as I put my son to bed and step out
again to watch the dark grow black
as the moon recedes, while somewhere east
the moon's already tipped her hat and you
have latched the latch and put the keys
in your pocket, whistling, clicking
down the street to your car, glancing back,
thinking that this is the only life
you'd ever wished for or dreamed.

Advice

First,
you've mistaken the crazy
for the mysterious. Strange-eyed
women with layers of feathers
or lace are not necessarily
hiding something.
If you must, search only
in the dark. Pick flowers.
Peel fruit. Dust.

Or look for a woman who hides
nothing. Look hard.
More than likely she's the one.
There is, of course, a price.
For a poem or two
she'll open her scars.
She'll sing to you all night
in the foreign tongue
of her womb. She'll fly.

Or look at that mirror.
The clue that lures you
lies between the glass
and the silver, between the shadow
and the ice. Do not move.
Open your eyes.

This

is the bread I make
and the bed I lie awake in.

It is the curtain
I pull to one side

when I want the stars
for friends. It is

the coin I spend
and the laundry

I wash over and over.
It is the rain I watch

and which I want
never to end.

There are times I wish
I could invite you,

and say, "Taste this,"
or say, "Try your head here."

But you have other places
to go. And this

is my place,
my travelling companion,

my one-woman show.

Dawn

This is the name
for the moment the quiet house
shifts between night and morning.

I sit in my swivel chair
in a room with two views, waiting
to catch it, the very moment.

Behind me the moon moves slowly down.
Before me the sky lightens,
and tree sounds change from frog

to bird. At first
the sun is an orange line
along the housetops.

Then it is a white ball,
and the moon
is gone.

This happens so fast
I've come dawn after dawn
to slow it down, to trap it.

I want to know what it is.
Not scientifically,
but with my whole body.

I want to know the precise moment
today became yesterday—
tomorrow, today. I want to say

I've gone deep enough,
that I've borrowed nothing,
that I've waited. But this is difficult.

I need to know so urgently exactly how
the woman who lies awake at night
becomes the sleeper, then the dreamer,

then the dream. I want to know why
the words I am saying seem to be spoken
by somebody else.

The sun is higher than my window now
and out of sight.
It is still winter.

I have to know what it's like
the moment that ice is not ice anymore
but isn't yet water.

Acknowledgments

House Without a Dreamer (1993 & 1995) and *The Other Life* (2001) were published by Story Line Press. *Woman in the Painting* (2006) was published by Autumn House Press. Grateful acknowledgement to both publishing houses for permission to reprint poems from these books.

And to the editors of the journals in which the following new poems were first published, much appreciation:

32 Poems: "On My Father's 87th Birthday"

Arts and Letters: "Question," "Overture," and "Wander"

Cloudbank: "New Year's Day"

FIELD: "Natural Causes"

The Georgia Review: "Blue," "Finches or Sparrows," "Portrait with Purple Shroud," and "Writing Studio"

The Gettysburg Review: "Afterwards"

In Posse Review: "Taffeta" and "Photograph of Her Grandmother as a Young Woman"

New Letters: "Kenmore Hotel, 1965" and "Large Boulder Above Honey River"

Snake Nation Review: "The Inconsolable"

Spillway: "Anniversary," "Desire," "Retrospective," "*American Gothic*," and "*Other*"

Trillium: "Every Time Her Husband Climbs a Ladder—"

The following poems were included in anthologies, websites, and textbooks:

"An Explanation" in *Conversation Pieces: Poems That Talk to Other Poems*. Kurt Brown, ed., Knopf (Everyman's Library Series), 2007

"Beauty Parlor" in *Art Beat*—The PBS News Hour website, 2009

"Firmly Married," "Living Room," "My Grandmother Taking Off My Grandfather's Shoes," "Nineteen-Thirty-Eight," and "When She Named Fire" in *When She Named Fire: An Anthology of Contemporary Poetry by American Women*, Andrea Hollander Budy, ed., Autumn House Press, 2009

"Dawn" in *Eco-songs: Poems for the Planet*. Peter Abbs, ed., Resurgence Press, 2002

"Delta Flight 1152," in *Air Fare*. Nickole Brown & Judith Taylor, eds. Sarabande Press, 2004

"Ex," "In the Garden," and "Nineteen-Thirty-Eight" in *The Autumn House Anthology of Contemporary American Poetry, 2nd edition*. Michael Simms, ed. Autumn House Press, 2011

"Finches or Sparrows" and "Large Boulder Above Honey River" in *Yonder Mountain: An Ozarks Anthology*. Anthony Priest, ed. University of Arkansas Press, 2013

"First Love" in *Poetry Calendar 2008*. Shafiq Naz, ed. Alhambra Publishing, 2007

"For Weeks After the Funeral" in *American Life in Poetry* (nationally syndicated newspaper column by Poet Laureate Ted Kooser)—January 25, 2007

"Getting Back," *Proposing on the Brooklyn Bridge: Poems About Marriage*. Ginny Lowe Connors, ed., Grayson Books, 2003

"Giving Birth" in *Writing Poems, 6th edition*. Robert Wallace and Michelle Boisseau, eds. Addison, Wesley, Longman, 2003

"How He Warmed Himself" *Southern California Poetry Anthology*, Issue 16 (1999)

"Hunters" (as "The Hunters") in *And What Rough Beast: Poems at the End of the Century*. Robert McGovern & Stephen Haven, eds. The Ashland Poetry Press, 1999; and in *The Autumn House Anthology of Contemporary American Poetry*. Sue Ellen Thompson, ed. Autumn House Press, 2005

"Living Room" won the 2004 *RUNES* Award, selected by Jane Hirshfield, and was later collected, along with "In the Sixth Year of My Father's Illness," in the anthology, *Lasting: Poems on Aging*. Meg Files, ed. Pima Press, 2005; and featured on *Art Beat*—The PBS News Hour website, 2009

"Nineteen-Thirty-Eight" on *The Writer's Almanac* (radio program by Garrison Keillor)—July 19, 2006

"Ochre" in *Poetry Calendar 2007*. Shafiq Naz, ed. Alhambra Publishing, 2006

"Permission" in *Don't Leave Hungry: Fifty Years of Southern Poetry Review*. James Smith, ed. University of Arkansas Press, 2009

"Pigs" in *The Lost Roads Project: A Walk-in Book of Arkansas*. C. D. Wright, ed., University of Arkansas Press, 1994

"Poem for My Brother, Manager of a Go-go Bar in Roselle Park, New Jersey" in *Night Out: Poems About Hotels, Motels, Restaurants, & Bars*. Kurt Brown & Laure-Anne Bosselaar, eds., Milkweed Editions, 1997

"Poem in October" in *The Autumn House Anthology of Contemporary American Poetry*. Sue Ellen Thompson, ed., Autumn House Press, 2005; and in *Beloved on the Earth: 150 Poems of Grief and Gratitude*. Jim Perlman, Deborah Cooper, Mara Hart, and Pamela Mittlefehldt, eds., Holy Cow! Press, 2009

"Reading Aloud to My Mother" and "My Father's Sweater" in *Are You Experienced? Baby Boom Poets at Midlife*. Pamela Gemin, ed., University of Iowa Press, 2005

"Remission" in *The Midwest Quarterly* 50:4 (Summer 2009)

"Snow White" in *The Poets' Grimm: Twentieth Century Poems from Grimm Fairy Tales*. Jeanne Marie Beaumont and Claudia Carlson, eds., Story Line Press, 2003; and in *Introduction to Poetry, 13th edition*, by Dana Gioia and X. J. Kennedy, Pearson Longman, 2009; and *Literature: An Introduction to Fiction, Poetry, Drama, and Writing (Series)* by Dana Gioia and X. J. Kennedy, Pearson Longman, 2009

"Sorrow" on *The Writer's Almanac* (radio program by Garrison Keillor) —July 12, 2012

"Soup" in *The Poet's Cookbook*. Sabine Pascarelli and Grace Cavalieri, eds., Bordighera Press, 2009, and (as "Stew") in *Like a Summer Peach*. Blanche Farley and Janice Moore, Eds., Papier-Maché Press, 1996

"Still Life with Jonquils" was featured on Poetry Daily (www.poems.com) on 10 September 2005; and in *Poetry Daily Essentials 2007*. Diane Boller and Don Selby, eds., Sourcebooks, 2007

"The Color of the Sky" in *Arkansas, Arkansas: Writers and Writings from the Delta to the Ozarks*. John Caldwell Guilds, ed., University of Arkansas Press, 1999

"Woman in the Painting" on *Poetry Daily*, July 22, 2006

"Writing Studio" in *Entering the Real World: VCCA Poets on Mt. San Angelo*. Margaret B. Ingraham and Andrea Carter Brown, eds., Wavertree Press, 2012

My appreciation for advice on poems previously published in earlier volumes was duly noted, and my debt to those individuals continues here. As for poems in the present volume: Much gratitude to the National Endowment for the Arts for a second fellowship (2007–2009), which provided much needed writing time, and to the Virginia Center for the Creative Arts, where some of the new poems in this volume were written during fellowships in 2008 and 2009. For meaningful support in the form of an annual writing semester, I am grateful to Lyon College. For valuable suggestions as I selected poems for this collection from earlier books, heartfelt thanks to Chana Bloch and Deborah Cummins. For helpful comments on individual poems-in-progress, gratitude to Lisa Bicmore, Chana Bloch, Margaret Chula, Stephen Corey, Christine Delea, Alice Friman, Cindy Williams Gutiérrez, Elizabeth Lacey Harris, Diane Holland, Paulann Petersen, Donna Prinzmetal, Paisley Rekdal, Joanna Rose, Natasha Sajé, Susan Sample, Penelope Scambly Schott, Suzanne Sigafoos, Jennifer Tonge, and the members of Poetry Group at First Unitarian Church of Portland. For invaluable tête-à-têtes as I finalized new poems, I am deeply indebted to John Brehm. And for his sensitive and wise counsel, I bow once more to Michael Simms, the kind of editor every writer wishes for.

The influence of three great teachers—John J. Clayton, Gregory Martin, and M. Lee Potts—none a teacher of the art and craft of poetry, is nevertheless present in everything I write.

Carol Christensen deserves special recognition for keeping me afloat when I most needed aid.

My deep gratitude to Sue Flemr for her enduring friendship that sustained me during a difficult transition.

For their immeasurable and enduring gifts I am wholly indebted to Brooke Budy, Avery Hill, Nisi Sturgis, Jordan Coughtry, and Robert Kirschenbaum.

Notes

On the epigraph that opens this volume—

> This seven-line excerpt is from the poem "Learning to Break the Rules,"
> which appeared in my chapbook, *What the Other Eye Sees* (Wayland
> Press, 1991).

On new poems in *Landscape with Female Figure*—

> "The Inconsolable" is for Evelyn Hollander.
> "Kenmore Hotel, 1965" is for Mark Weinberger.
> The poem by John Brehm referred to in "Question" is "Some Clouds
> Some Questions" from his *Sea of Faith* (University of Wisconsin Press,
> 2004).

On the poems in *Woman in the Painting*—

> "In the Garden" is for Judith Burnley.
> Line 1 of "Spark" comes from Philip Levine's "My Son and I."
> "Living Room" is for Evelyn Hollander and in memory of Milton
> Hollander.
> "Remission" was written for Kathleen Lynch.

On the poems in *The Other Life*—

> "Those Summer Sundays" is in response to Robert Hayden's "Those
> Winter Sundays."
> Line 9 of "Afterwards" is from Philip Larkin's "Talking in Bed."
> "An Explanation" is in response to Stephen Dunn's "Missing."
> The first line of "What I Need It For" is a variation on one from
> Stephen Sandy's "A Bamboo Brushpot."
> "Woman and Husband" is in the voice of the woman in Robert Lowell's
> "Man and Wife."

On the poems in *House Without a Dreamer*—

"Choice" is for Estelle Berlin and Sarah Warner.

"When You Hear His Name" is for Richard Silverlieb.

"Firmly Married" was written for Loretta Price.

"What I Want" is for Diane Tebbetts.

"Poem for My Brother, Manager of a Go-go Bar in Roselle Park, New Jersey" was written for Gordon Hollander.

"Advice" was written for Doren Robbins.

Index of Titles and First Lines

The Autumn House Poetry Series

Michael Simms, General Editor

OneOnOne	Jack Myers
Snow White Horses	Ed Ochester
The Leaving	Sue Ellen Thompson
Dirt	Jo McDougall
Fire in the Orchard	Gary Margolis
Just Once: New and Previous Poems	Samuel Hazo
The White Calf Kicks	Deborah Slicer • 2003, selected by Naomi Shihab Nye
The Divine Salt	Peter Blair
The Dark Takes Aim	Julie Suk
Satisfied with Havoc	Jo McDougall
Half Lives	Richard Jackson
Not God After All	Gerald Stern
Dear Good Naked Morning	Ruth L. Schwartz • 2004, selected by Alicia Ostriker
A Flight to Elsewhere	Samuel Hazo
Collected Poems	Patricia Dobler
The Autumn House Anthology of Contemporary American Poetry	Sue Ellen Thompson, ed.
Déjà Vu Diner	Leonard Gontarek
lucky wreck	Ada Limón • 2005, selected by Jean Valentine
The Golden Hour	Sue Ellen Thompson
Woman in the Painting	Andrea Hollander Budy
Joyful Noise: An Anthology of American Spiritual Poetry	Robert Strong, ed.

• Winner of the annual Autumn House Poetry Prize

* *Coal Hill Review* chapbook series

Design and Production

Text and cover design: Chiquita Babb

Cover painting: Brooke Budy

Author photograph: Brooke Budy

This book is typeset in Monotype Centaur, a Humanist type family designed by Bruce Rogers. Centaur, originally drawn in 1914 for the Metropolitan Museum of Art as titling capitals, is based on several Renaissance models, primarily one by Nicholas Jensen. Rogers later added the lower case roman letters. The italic was drawn in 1925 by Frederic Warde, based on a font by Ludovico Arrighi. Centaur was released for general use in 1929.

This book was printed by McNaughton & Gunn on 55# Glatfelter Natural